AF417929

Matters of the Heart
A 31 Day Devotional
To Encourage Your Heart

Dr. Deborah A. Vails

Women of Power Ministries, Inc.
Van Buren, Arkansas

INTRODUCTION

Matters of the Heart was birthed out of a 31-day prayer focus that the Lord led me to do in December 2018. Each day the Lord gave me a theme on the heart after each prayer I wrote. At the time, I had no idea that I would write a devotional from these themes.

In August 2019 the Lord spoke to me that I was to write a devotional entitled "*Matters of the Heart*". It is my prayer that each devotional will minister to you in a special way. Keep in mind, these devotionals are straight from the heart of God.

Who better to speak into your life than God the Father, creator of heaven and earth. I pray the blessing of the Lord be upon you as you read each day!

Be Blessed,
Dr. Deborah Vails
October 12, 2019

Day 1
A Heart of Love

True love will flow from your heart when you submit it to God. Jesus displayed His love for you by giving His all in order that you would know His enduring love, compassion, mercy and grace.

A heart that loves gives without fear or reservation.

A heart that loves serves, is kind, good, merciful, gentle and sincere.

A heart that loves freely forgives and does not keep track of wrongs or injustices. A heart of love freely gives all.

I encourage you to allow the Lord to pour His love into your heart so that you, in turn can pour out pure enduring love to others. Trust God with your whole heart, he will not disappoint you.

Scriptures to ignite you:

1 Corinthians 13:1-13

Day 2
A Heart that Cares

Life can carry the potential for one to become cold and callous due to hard hits that affect your heart. Jesus was hit hard by rejection, ridicule, scandalous words, character assassination and defamation. He did not allow any of these things to remove the caring, loving attitude he displayed for us from His heart.

A heart that cares looks for ways to help those who are bitter, miserable, mean and hateful.

A heart that cares goes above and beyond to please God in all manner of living, behavior and attitude.

A heart that cares will put others first, and will keep God at the helm of their life.

I encourage you to push forward and allow the Lord to reveal His caring heart to you so that you can implement His caring love to others.

Scriptures to ignite you:

1 Peter 5:7

Day 3
A Heart That is Sincere

Joseph was a young man when he found himself in a terrible position. He brothers turned on him, stripped him of his coat and threw him in a pit, leaving him to die. He was later sold into slavery. No doubt he questioned why God would allow his own family to turn on him. The heart of his brothers was sincere about carrying out this wrong against their own.

Joseph learned the value of being sincere with no hidden motive or agenda to get even years later when his brothers arrived in Egypt for food. When he saw his brothers his heart broke as they waited expectantly for help, not realizing they were speaking to their brother who was calling the shots. They would soon find out the sincerity that Joseph had.

A heart that is sincere will carry out the instructions God gives with no hidden motives. A heart that is sincere is completely transparent.

A sincere heart will cause you to walk in freedom and liberty, God will also give you the ability to live above reproach.

Joseph realized Gods plan for his life, to bring deliverance to his family. Even though it looked like his brothers were out to see him dead, God had other plans.

Beloved, there is a greater plan for your life, keep a sincere heart in all you do. This will ensure that you remain pure and clean.

Scriptures to ignite you:

Genesis 37-50 2 Corinthians 1:12

Day 4
A Heart That Remembers

Many things happen in our lives in which we do not wish to remember. A heart that remembers rejects the negative, opens up for the positive to remain in order to thrive in health and wholeness.

A heart that remembers applies discretion, wisdom and knowledge. A heart that remembers appreciates the small things, shows gratitude and remains connected to healthy streams. A heart that remembers will give to the one who may need to see and experience love of God through you.

I encourage you to remember what God has and continues to do for you. Remember God is watching over His word for you. Do something special for someone today that will show that you truly do remember.

Scriptures to ignite you:

Psalm 78:35 Psalm 98:3

Day 5
A Heart That Prays

Prayer is one of the most important things that must be a part of your everyday life.

Jesus is the best example of one who was consistent and diligent to pray regularly.

Without prayer, you will be weak in your Christian walk. In order for prayer to be effective it must be done from the heart. It involves getting to know the Lord personally. It involves communicating with God and allowing Him to be an active part of your life.

Prayer involves three things:

Asking – bringing your issues to God

Seeking – enquiring of Him to get to know the Lord better

Knocking – God calls you to come close to Him so He can share His heart with you

As you learn to go into the throne room with God, you will learn what it means to abide in and dwell with Him.

God longs to fellowship with you beloved. Develop a heart that prays, in doing this, you will learn how to stay in His presence.

God will fill your heart with overflowing love from Him. God desires that you have a heart that prays.

Scriptures to ignite you:

Matthew 7:7-8

Psalm 16:11 Matthew 11:28-29

Day 6
A Heart That Forgives

Forgiveness is something we have all struggled with at one time or another. Jesus spoke plainly about forgiveness.

A heart that forgives does not keep track of wrongs. A heart that forgives will release those that have hurt or offended them quickly.

Jesus stated in His word that if you do not forgive neither will your Father in Heaven forgive you. In order to walk in freedom, you must be willing to forgive totally.

A heart that forgives is one that is truly free, pure and clean. The word of God will help to clean you up in this area.

Beloved, many times people may do things to you and yes, it is a travesty but they have no idea what they are doing. There is power in forgiveness. The power you have is the ability to release, move forward, walk free and stay free because of the work Jesus has done for you.

I encourage you to allow the Lord to explore the areas in your life that may be held up due to unforgiveness. Let go of those issues that have held you in bondage. Follow the example that Jesus gave, the power of forgiveness will keep you free and it will keep the swinging door of the enemy jammed!

Scriptures to ignite you:

Matthew 6:24-15 Matthew 18:21-35 Mark 11:25-26

I encourage you to allow the Lord to explore the areas in your life that may be held up due to unforgiveness. Let go of those issues that have held you in bondage. Follow the example that Jesus gave, the power of forgiveness will keep you free and it will keep the swinging door of the enemy jammed!

Scriptures to ignite you:

Matthew 6:24-15 Matthew 18:21-35 Mark 11:25-26

Day 7
A Heart That Stewards Well

When a person is given a job to do and entrusted with duties that may include overseeing a home, finances or trusts, to name a few, that person is a steward.

When the Master gave the talents and went his way, he trusted those in charge of what He gave them to make a profit. Two of them were faithful, one was not. As a result, he lost what he had along with his position.

A heart that stewards well has a sharp attention to detail, is obedient, faithful and committed. One of the most important things the Lord is looking for is faithfulness.

I encourage you to make sure you are a good steward of everything God has placed in your hands. God has entrusted you and He will help you to take care of all that is in your hands.

Continue to lean and depend on the Lord, He will not fail you, He will help you with all He has called you to do.

Scriptures to ignite you:

1 Corinthians 4:2

Day 8
A Heart That is Wise

At times, it takes experience to learn wisdom. The Bible is full of scriptures on wisdom, when you apply wisdom and walk in it, your heart will become complete.

A heart that is wise will cause you to think before reacting to situations that may cause you trouble.

A heart that is wise will look to the Lord for guidance, direction, instruction and knowledge. A heart that is wise will apply discretion, will learn to be slow to speak, quick to hear and always ready to heed the voice of the Lord.

A heart that is wise will teach others to walk worthy of their vocation and press forward in order to reach the goal.

I encourage you to seek the Lord and apply His wisdom to your heart. As you do this, He will perfect those things that concern you. Abide in His wisdom and He will cause you to flourish in all that you put your hands to do.

Scriptures to ignite you:
Proverbs 2:1-22

Day 9
A Heart That is Healthy

The Lord says, I desire that you prosper and walk in health. As you submit your heart to me, I will purify, I will cleanse and I will heal you.

Walk in my word and know that I will continue to lead, guide and direct you by my spirit. I the Lord will watch over my word and I will cause you to walk in pure health as you surrender all to me.

I will heal you of all past hurts, trauma, disappointments and all that has hindered your progress. Keep your eyes on me and know that I will cause your health to spring forth speedily says the Lord.

Scriptures to ignite you:

3 John 2 Proverbs 4:23

Day 10
A Heart of Integrity

The Bible talks about integrity in Psalm 26:1-12. Let's begin by defining integrity.

Integrity – means to be complete, full, whole, sound, innocent and perfect (Psalm 26:1 Proverbs 10:9).

A heart of integrity will allow the Lord to search or try according to Psalm 26:2 which says, *Examine me O Lord and prove me; try my reins and my heart.* When things are not right, allow the Lord to put you to the test to ensure you maintain your integrity.

A heart of integrity remembers God love. Psalm 26:3-5 says, *For thy loving kindness is before mine eyes: and I have walked in thy truth. I have not sat with vain persons; neither will I go in with dissemblers. I have hated the congregation of evil doers; and will not sit with the wicked.*

Remember Gods love toward you, when you have walk upright before God you can remind Him of His word, He will hear you.

A heart of integrity will allow cleansing and will be placed on the altar. Psalm 26:6-7 reads, *I will wash my hands in innocency: so will I compass thing altar, O Lord: that I may publish with the voice of thanksgiving, and tell of all thy wondrous works.*

A heart of integrity will be committed to walk with the Lord. Psalm 26:8-12 states, LORD I have loved the habitation of thy house, and the place where thine honour dwelleth. Gather not my soul with sinners, nor my life with bloody men: In whose hands *is* mischief, and their right hand is full of bribes. But as for me, I will walk in mine integrity: redeem me, and be merciful unto me. My foot standeth in an even place: in the congregations will I bless the LORD.

I encourage you to walk in integrity even when things hit you that cause pain. Allow the Lord to minister to you in the areas no one knows about. Be honest before Him and watch Him move for you!

Scriptures to ignite you:

1 Corinthians 10:13

Day 11
A Heart of Peace

Several years ago, I walked through a very difficult time that included an illness where the doctors could not get to the root of the problem. I lost a lot of weight and it seemed that my strength left my body. It continued for months and it felt as if I would not recover.

I remember laying in the hospital and the peace of God walked in my room. I felt the Lord standing at the foot of my bed and I knew I would be okay. I actually got worse before I got better.

After going home, one day I looked to my right while laying in my bed and there the Lord appeared to me. Once again, I felt such a peace, I really cannot explain it but I knew I would be okay. It would be a few more weeks before my strength began to return.

As I reflect on that time the Lord ministered to me that His peace will keep your heart. Knowing that no matter what situation you may face the peace of God will walk with you has really helped me weather storms that I do not believe I would have been able to endure.

Beloved, God will give you a heart of peace every day. When you have His peace, you know that you are on the right track, no matter what is taking place.

If you are struggling and you have no peace take time to get before the Lord, allow Him to minister to you, repent of anything that He shows you that is sin. Having a heart of peace will help you endure and walk through every trial you may be called to face.

Beloved, God will give you a heart of peace every day. When you have His peace, you know that you are on the right track, no matter what is taking place.

If you are struggling, and have no peace, take time to get before the Lord, allow Him to minister to you, repent of anything that He shows you that is sin. Having a heart of peace will help you endure and walk through every trial you may be called to face.

The Lord says, I have come to heal every wound, I have come to remove discouragement, disappointment, sadness, hopelessness, loneliness and despair.

Trust me, yield to me, know that I have come to set you free.

Surrender your all to me for I am the Lord your God and I change not. Allow my peace to flood your heart, mind, soul and body. I will walk with you as you continue to walk with me. Give me your worries, fears and cares and I will give you renewed strength.

Come out of all that has held you bound and know that I will cleanse, refresh and make you whole says the Lord.

Scriptures to ignite you:

1 Peter 5:7 Philippians 4:6-8

Day 12
A Heart That is Motivated

A heart that is motivated is one that is provoked to love and good works. Love will motivate you to be kind, compassionate, sincere and good.

A heart that is motivated will provoke others to walk as Jesus does, be all Jesus desires them to be and will not waver but will be strong in faith.

A heart that is motivated will face each day with excitement, enthusiasm and joy knowing that God will do great things.

A heart that is motivated understands the joy that God gives and the strength that causes one to endure.

I encourage you to keep motivated, do not stop, quit or slow your roll! God is on your side; you will make it!

Scriptures to ignite you:

Lamentations 3:22-25 Isaiah 40:29-31

Day 13
A Heart That is Obedient

The Bible states that if you are willing and obedient you will eat the good of the land (Isaiah 1:19).

A heart that is obedient will accept the Lord and all that has been provided by Him, will continue to seek to obey God in all He commands.

A heart that is obedient will walk in the love of God, upright before Him, accept His order, that He may work a complete work in you.

A heart that is obedient will reap the benefits of a Christ like life and will be fulfilled in every area.

I encourage you to continue to keep an obedient heart, keep watch and remain alert. Do not allow the enemy to plant seeds of disobedience in your life because it could cause you to be devoured by the sword. Strive to be quick to obey the Lord.

Scriptures to ignite you:

Isaiah 1:19-20

Day 14
A Heart That is Friendly

In order to have friends one must show himself friendly. Often times, you may be hesitant to open up to those you do not know.

Jesus showed us how to be friendly when he befriended those who were sinners and considered outcasts. Instead of judging them He took time to share with them.

A heart that is friendly will be genuine, real and true. Will not pretend or put on a show. Will not be brash, harsh or rude. Will not have a suspicious eye but will seek to help those who need a listening ear.

Beloved, you may need a friend, someone who understands. Jesus will be that kind of friend to you. He will listen to you, answer your questions and give you the hope and strength to reach out to others. Allow the Lord to give you what you need each day to be a good friend.

Scriptures to ignite you: Proverbs

18:24 Matthew 9:9-13

Day 15
Heart That is Pure

It is a blessing to see one who is truly pure. A heart that is pure is one that is clear and clean with no contaminates.

A heart that is pure seeks after God, has a desire to do and walk after Him.

A heart that is pure has no hidden motives or agendas. A heart that is pure seeks to remain clean in order to be used by God in the fullest and most complete way possible.

As you seek after God, He will help you to maintain a pure heart.

I encourage you to run after God, He will strengthen your heart and make you whole.

Scriptures to ignite you:

Matthew 5:1-12

Day 16
A Heart That Desires God

Psalms 37:4 says, Delight thyself also in the Lord; and he shall give thee the desires of thine heart.

A heart that desires God will seek after Him, petition Him and will receive what is asked for.

A heart that desires God delights in Him, keeping Him first and foremost. It is Gods will to bless, honor and give you what you need and also desire.

As you learn to give your heart over to God, trust that He knows what to do, desire more of Him and He will satisfy every part of your life.

Take delight in Him and His word and watch Him cause you to gain all you need to fulfill your destiny.

Scriptures to ignite you:
Psalm 37:3-6 Psalm 34:8-9

Day 17
A Heart That is Diligent

Wherefore, beloved, seeing that ye look for such things, be diligent that ye may be found of him in peace, without spot, and blameless (2 Peter 3:14).

A heart that is diligent is one that is prompt, earnest and endeavors to labor to be found in the Lord preparing for His coming.

A heart that is diligent is constant in pursuit for more of God.

A heart that is diligent will watch and pray to avoid falling into temptation and sin. Realizing that as the end approaches the reality to cast off the works of darkness is paramount as evil increases in the land.

I encourage you to guard your heart, so that the life that flows from you remains pure. Be diligent to push forward, leave the past behind you. There is more that God has for you beloved, let His peace be found in you completely!

Scriptures to ignite you:

Proverbs 4:23 Psalm 119:34

Day 18
A Heart That Respects

A heart that respects is one that reveres, honors, submits and obeys. To revere is to reverence, to honor and acknowledge, to submit, to respect and to obey, to simply do the right thing.

A heart that respects will put to practice these things for the glory and honor of God.

I encourage you to reverence Gods presence at all times.   When you do this, He is welcomed into your everyday life and walk. God will not only walk with you; He will be found of you the hope of glory and He will manifest His presence in and through your life.

Scriptures to ignite you:

Psalm 40:4 Psalm 119:15, 17

Day 19
A Heart of Compassion

A heart of compassion is filled with love. It takes compassion to love the unlovable, to be good and gentle to those who are unloving.

A heart of compassion sees the good and because of love will see ways of victory out of dark situations or circumstances.

Jesus walked and flowed out of a heart of compassion. His love caused Him to endure rejection, chastisement, ridicule and death so that mankind would be free.

When you flow from a heart that is full of compassion the love of God will flow to those in need.

I encourage you to allow the love and compassion of the Lord to have first place in your life. In doing this, mankind will see Jesus lifted up and the power of God will be manifested in the earth realm.

Scriptures to ignite you:

Isaiah 53: 1-5

Day 20
The Heart of a Warrior

Joshua was a man who served the Lord by receiving the residue of the presence of God on the mountain. He experienced times of war but His heart was to please God and serve Moses as best he could.

He went from servant to leader but the heart of the warrior remained in him.

When you have the heart of a warrior you will learn to fight with different weapons that, if sharp, will get the job done.

The heart of a warrior will stand in the face of battle. The heart of a warrior will face the opponent with confidence that God will give wisdom on how to bring him down.

The heart of the warrior will stay in the fight, will not retreat or run, even when it appears that defeat is near.

I encourage you to keep the heart of a warrior, pray in the spirit daily, and stay built up, in doing this you will hear the Lord with clarity and will know how to proceed in order that victory is won!

Scriptures to ignite you:

Exodus 17:1-16 1 Samuel 30:8

Day 21
The Heart of a Leader

God calls and qualifies who He chooses for leadership. He knows your makeup and the abilities He has placed in you. As He develops you, He will teach you how to walk in order to be effective in His Kingdom.

In his book, The Making of a Leader, Frank Damazio defines the word *"heart" as "the seat of man's collective energies and the focus of his personal life. He also states that the heart is the throne that life itself sits. When the Lord asks for a man's heart, He wants that person to be involved in the Lord's work from the very core of his being."*

The heart of a leader will grieve over sin in the body of Christ. The heart of a leader will remain faithful in difficulties (Nehemiah 6:3).

The heart of a leader will pant after God

(Psalm 42:1).

I encourage you to be all God has called you to be, do all God has called you to do, and live every day to please and complete every assignment that God gives.

Pour your heart out to the Lord so that He can fill you new and fresh each day. Above all, remember God has called you to a holy calling, He will see that you walk in the destiny He has ordained for you.

Scriptures to ignite you:

Proverbs 3:1-8

Day 22
A Heart That Gives

A heart that gives does so without reservation or grief (Deuteronomy 15:10). We have all heard many sermons and exhortations on giving. The Bible is clear that when you give it should be done without a grudge or of necessity. This will produce fruit in your life.

A heart that gives will share willingly, in order for others to receive what they need. As you learn to link with God in this area your life will never lack or want any good or beneficial thing.

Keep an open heart to give, not only of your substance, but from every area that God directs you to give from. May the abundance of God always flow as you learn the secret of giving from your heart.

Scriptures to ignite you:

2 Corinthians 9:1-15

Day 23
A Heart That Understands

We serve a God who understands who we are and who delights in us getting to know and understand Him.

A heart that understands can instruct others in various ways, guide when needed and teach with wisdom so others can gain the knowledge needed to know God better.

A heart that understands is willing to show mercy and grace to those who may not deserve it so that the glory of the Lord be displayed and the drawing of the Holy Spirit may minister to the one in need.

Ephesians 5:17 Ephesians 3:14-19

Day 24
A Heart That is Content

Paul was a man that suffered much during his walk with the Lord. He stated that whatever state he found himself in he would be content (Philippians 4:11).

A heart that is content will not murmur or complain. A heart that is content will look for ways to adjust to each situation that one is called to face.

A heart that is content will not slack off from the call or ministry God has given. A heart that is content will be motivated to move forward despite the difficulties or challenges one is called to face.

I encourage you to look to the hills for this is where your help will come from. Do not allow the enemy to give you a spirit of heaviness, praise the name of the Lord and watch God move for you.

Scriptures to ignite you:

Psalm 121:1-8

Day 25
A Heart That is Pliable

God sent Jeremiah down to the Potter's house so that He could speak to him there. When he got there, he saw the potter on the wheel and there was clay on the potter's wheel. He was attempting to make a vessel.

A heart that is pliable is one who does not tell the Lord how, why, when or what to do. A heart that is pliable does not have a voice as to what God wants done or how He plans to do it.

A heart that is pliable is sold out to the Lord and has no fear of what the future may hold.

A heart that is pliable will allow the potter to make the vessel of His choice and will be led by the Spirit of the Lord without fear or reservation.

Allow the Lord to make you after His image, develop you for effective service, and pour into you over and over again so that you become the vessel meet for the master's use.

Scriptures to ignite you:
Jeremiah 18:1-23 2 Timothy 2:19-21

Day 26
A Heart Filled with Purpose

Daniel was a man of purpose that served God in purity and holiness. He was determined not to be defiled by the king's meat. This would prove beneficial for him and the Hebrew boys.

God also gives purpose to those called to ministry. A heart filled with purpose will have vision from God, will endeavor to complete His will and will not be afraid to walk in all that God has.

A heart filled with purpose will encourage others to fulfill their God given dreams and visions.

God's divine purpose in your life will keep you moving, viable and vital in the Kingdom of God.

I encourage you not to let down on anything God has given you to do. Continue to move forward, do not get stuck or procrastinate, do all God gives you to do, run your race with intensity. Go for the goal, know that you are a winner and God will give you complete victory!

Scriptures to ignite you: Daniel

1:1-21 Philippians 3:7-15

Day 27
A Heart That is Subject

A heart that is subject is obedient, respectful and submissive, obedient to all God requires and says, respectful and reverent to Him and submissive to His word and will.

A heart that is subject will submit to authority without resistance. A heart that is subject will keep account of one's actions to ensure the free flow of the Holy Spirit in all manner of living.

The Lord calls us to submit to His word by heeding and being a doer of it.

True humility will keep you from pride and self-elevation. The love of God will flow from you, as you remain subject and humble before the Lord. Be determined to keep a heart that is subject.

Scriptures to ignite you:

James 1:22-23

Day 28
A Heart That is Mature

The Bible says as new born babes desire the sincere milk of the word that you may grow thereby (1 Peter 2:2). Babes are not able to digest meat but as they develop and grow, they are able to take in more nourishment.

A heart that is mature will not handle situations like a child, but will use wisdom, knowledge and understanding from the word of God.

A heart that is mature will continually grow and develop into the full stature of Jesus Christ.

I encourage you to allow the Lord to expand you in every area of your life. God has so much for you as you allow Him to grow and perfect you. All Him to complete, mature and make you whole.

Psalm 138:8 I John 4:17

Day 29
A Heart of Expectation

Paul was a man that lived with expectation that whether he lived or died Christ would be magnified.

A heart of expectation lives to please God, hungers for His presence, and abides under His shadow.

The Bible says, if you hunger and thirst after righteousness you will be filled (Matthew 5:6). Abiding in His presence provides protection, refuge and safety from the enemies blows.

A heart of expectation will be quick to get rid of sin, and will remain in a place where healing and deliverance is a constant in your life.

There is no better place to reside than in the presence of the Lord. Keep a heart of expectation and watch God move in ways in your life that will astound you more and more.

Scriptures to ignite:

Psalm 91:1-16 Philippians 1:1-30 Psalm 16:11

Day 30
A Heart of Unity

Behold, how good and how pleasant it is for brethren to dwell together in unity! It is like the precious ointment upon the head, that ran down upon the beard, even Aaron's beard: that went down to the skirts of his garments; As the dew of Hermon, and as the dew that descended upon the mountains of Zion: for there the LORD commanded the blessing, even life for evermore (Psalm 133:1-3).

It is awesome when brethren can come together in unity. A heart of unity strives with others for the same purpose of the gospel.

To strive means to be in company with, to partner together for the same purpose so the will of God is completed in the earth.

I encourage you to keep unity with one another. Do not allow the enemy to divide you with discord, dissention or gossip. Always speak well of one another and allow the love of God abide in and through.

Scriptures to ignite you:

Hebrews 13:1-25

Day 31
A Heart That Cleaves

God the creator of marriage desires that husband and wife truly cleave to one another.

A heart that cleaves clings, adheres, pursues and sticks close to one another.

A heart that cleaves will not leave when things gets rough, will not quit in the midst of battle and will not give up when things look bleak.

Whether you are married or single, you must have a heart that cleaves. Pursue hard after God, He will not fail nor forsake you. He will give you what you need to push ahead.

I encourage you to keep yourself in the love of God, keep your heart surrendered to Him, and do not allow your momentum to wane. Remember, God is faithful that promised, so hold on to His word and cleave close to Him.

Genesis 2:21-25 Joel 2:21-27

References

Dake, Finis. (1949). *Gods Plan for Man*. Lawrenceville, Georgia, USA: Dake Bible Sales.

Damazio, Frank. (1988). *The Making of a Leader*. Portland, Oregon, USA: City Bible Publishing.

Vails, Deborah. (2018). *Devotions from the Fathers Heart*.

Van Buren, Arkansas, USA: Women of Power Ministries, Inc.

To learn more about Set Free Outreach Ministries or for
speaking engagements contact us at:

Set Free Outreach Ministries
P.O. Box 1533
Van Buren, Arkansas 72957

Visit us on the website:
www.setfreeoutreachministries.org

Publications by Dr. Deborah Vails

Devotions from the Fathers Heart
I'm Covered
Defeating the Spirit of Sabotage
How to Keep Going Under Pressure
The Clashing of the Swords
A Walk Through the Book of Proverbs
The Body Was Made to House Not to Lead
The Healing Manual